Learning How to Walk

Jim Jackson

ISBN 979-8-89112-516-2 (Paperback)
ISBN 979-8-89112-517-9 (Digital)

Covenant Books
11661 Hwy 707
Murrells Inlet, SC 29576
www.covenantbooks.com

Author taking some of his first steps

And Enoch walked with God. (Genesis 5:24)

From the day I was born, I was provided with good transportation, either on feet or on wheels.

Author waiting beside the family car

The spirit of the living creature was in the wheels.
(Ezekiel 1:20)

By 1947, I was five years old. The Sabine River was flowing past our home less than a mile away. Mama's '38 Ford was having some trouble getting us to town on the muddy road.

Daddy and Mommy, James and Maggie Jackson 1940
(mommy's 1938 Ford is in the background)

Daddy had given his Model A Ford to Uncle Lee and was driving a 1938 Chevy pickup, mostly for use on the farm.

Then one day, it arrived, a Willis Jeep with a canvas top and no frills, but it had two amazing features: four-wheel drive and mud-grip tires.

Later, my dad bought an aluminum cab and replaced the canvas top with that. It was surely a nice improvement, especially during winter or when it was raining.

Willis Jeep with aluminum top in background, my sister
Margaret Ann and my pet goat Billy, are pictured with me

And later, my dad bought a 1941 Mercury coupe, which we drove to the river one day to go fishing. The battery was weak, and the engine needed a tune-up, so my dad parked on a hill where he could roll down the hill and start the engine.

Our transportation needs occasionally experienced some hardships and limitations, but usually we arrived at the place where we needed to go. And it did require some experience and knowledge and imagination to find a good fishing location near a hill.

But fishing was a high priority some days in the world that my dad grew up in, not just for sport but because somebody was hungry. (Fishing is important in the Bible too. As we are told, Jesus chose Peter, a fisherman, for one of his main helpers.)

James Jackson, my dad, doing what he loved best --- fishing

Another time, according to my dad, some fishermen were able to get safely back home using pork fat, cooking oil, in their engine, after losing their engine oil due to a sudden accidental leak in their oil pan.

They ran over something in the road and knocked the plug out of the pan. This required the special woodworking skills of a fisherman who could carve another oil pan plug out of a tree limb.

Another wheeled vehicle activity in my life was riding in passenger trains from early childhood into the 1970s.

My lifework plans, for some odd reason, never included working for the railroad. I don't understand why, but it may have been due to the sudden uncertain and unexpected process which was overtaking the main system, changing the drive power from steam to diesel engines.

And I even studied and worked on diesel locomotive engines as an oil field mechanic during the 1960s.

My dad, my uncles, and my other relatives all worked for Texas and Pacific, Missouri Pacific, and others when train riding was in style.

But car riding for everyone seems to have become more convenient and popular and personal and not so old fashioned. This may prove to be a very sad and costly mistake for the future of our modern world.

Steam engine, San Antonio, TX, 2015

Mommy worked for the government, helping poor farmers fill out their forms to get some money. Daddy was always busy on the farm, so a neighbor was hired for childcare.

Friend Vera and mommy, Maggie Jackson, at her office, 1952

My babysitter used a lot of profanity or cuss words, as they were called, and one day I used one of those words in front of my grandmother.

This resulted in one of the worst whippings that my grandmother ever gave me. Probably, a cussing grandson would not be appreciated by one of the founding members of the local Baptist church.

> Let all...evil speaking...be put away from you.
> (Ephesians 4:31)

We called my grandmother Mammaw. She was my main babysitter most of the time. And she would talk to me and tell me true stories about relatives who had died.

Beulah Virginia/Virgie Grimmer Jackson was
called Mammaw by our family

From the age of five until the age of twenty, I was steered away from evil and danger numerous times. Frustration, disappointment, sadness, and other negatives would accompany me too, but generally, those years were blessed.

He helped me learn how to drive a tractor when I was six years old. I will always thank Valdon, who was helping my dad with our hay-harvesting work.

Valdon lifted me up, one day, in front of him, where I could grip the steering wheel of our tractor, a Ford-Ferguson 9N.

My legs were not long enough yet to reach the clutch and brake pedals, so Valdon worked them, but I could surely steer the tractor and move the throttle lever, which was located beneath the steering wheel. Thank You, Lord, for such useful training, so early in my life.

Ford-Ferguson 9N tractor

My cousin Louis had a Studebaker pickup, which he let me drive, although I could barely see over the steering wheel. He also had a mare with a colt, and one day he let me go for a ride on her.

She was still very wide from giving birth. I was riding bareback (with no saddle). After wandering a considerable distance from the barn, she became aware of a noise and raised her ears.

Oh no, the colt was calling for his mama. She took off, running toward the barn. When I pulled on the reins, it didn't stop her. And trying to grip her mane was not enough. All I could do was lay over, try to put my arms around her neck, and hold on tight. Otherwise, I would have fallen off.

What a scary event for a young cowboy, and it wasn't too long before another horse, which belonged to a friend, also ran away with me.

These two runaway horse events altered my cowboy plans for the rest of my life. The horse you are riding must respect your wishes to sit on their back and your efforts to control them. (Just ask any rodeo person if you don't believe this.)

Cowboy Jimmy and Mammaw, 1950

My friend Don had a 1933 Plymouth coupe with a strong V-8 Chevy engine. It was an attractive body style with a very powerful engine. One day as he was driving us home from a racing event, it started raining.

Not realizing how slick the highway had suddenly become, he started to pass another car. Suddenly the back wheels lost traction, and the rear of the car started coming around.

Then the car started spinning around like a top in the middle of a section of highway that had steep embankments on both sides. After several spins, it slid off the pavement at a point where the road was not so steep.

For a considerable distance, it slid sideways, taking out a mailbox on a post, breaking loose the exhaust pipes, and getting covered with mud.

Thankfully, Don was able to drive up out of the ditch and then drive us home. Does our God warn us about future dangers? No question, He does.

Motorcycle wishes also entered my thoughts as a young boy. Going on some test rides and furnishing my wardrobe with the black leather jacket and boots that bikers wore, I purchased a worn-out Harley. Money was needed and special skills, but my plans were interrupted one night.

Having a terrible wreck was an event that I had not considered in my hopes for two-wheeled transportation. But this was the subject of a very frightening dream that I had about riding a motorcycle. I dreamt that I had a serious accident.

> God…speaks to man…in a dream…and…seals instructions…to protect him. (Job 33:14–16)

The serous nature of this choice was further emphasized by the tragic deaths of two of my favorite musicians in the 1970s.

> Take me home…if you don't know that…I shouldn't be having a date with you.!

Thus it ended, another failed attempt to have a girlfriend when I was in high school.

My upbringing in the Baptist Church had taught me that Jesus Christ was my personal savior, available now, 24-7, or whenever I need Him.

Never had I ever been misled to believe that Jesus was just another one of those "saints" up in heaven and the subject of a cheap jewelry item to be worn on a chain around the neck.

All I did was to ask a Catholic girl about her "Saint Christopher" medal, as we drove away from her house on our first date.

Thank You, Lord, for delivering me and protecting me from such evil, human-designed heresy and abomination.

When my granddad, A. M. Jackson died in 1940, a big crowd of people came to his funeral, and the white people were very much outnumbered.

Andrew Martin Jackson, my grand-dad with his Bible, 1900

No refrigerators were available during those times, and the cow always provided more milk than the family needed, so it was my dad's job to carry a bucket of fresh milk down the road and give it to the neighbors.

Wherever we lived, we always had a starving bunch of them close by us, according to Mammaw. Like members of our family, sharing food, providing work and a place to live. Nothing but friendly words and deeds for many years.

John's wife, Lula, had died and John himself was getting old and still living alone in a small house by the creek. My dad offered John a better place to live near our house, which he took for a short while, until his daughter came and took him with her.

While John was with us, he did some childcare for me while Mommy was at the office. And one day he decided to prepare a meal for us. He worked on our meal for a long time and really put some effort into it. And soon we sat down to eat, and what did he prepare? It was one of his favorites, sweet potatoes and possum.

Growing up in a rural area in Tennessee, Mommy had heard a lot of country music and eventually disliked it a lot. In fact, she hated it.

Consequently, one day when my cowboy heart wanted to sing some western songs, I asked Mommy if I could have a guitar.

No, she said, "I don't want you playing and singing country music." Instead, she paid for me to take piano lessons. The pain and disappointment from this experience never went away.

And to further guarantee this situation, I injured my left arm and would never be able to make the chords that guitar playing would require.

For vengeance, I bought and listened to guitar music for the rest of my life. I especially enjoyed the "stretched strings" of blues songs mixed with rock, and the sad music of Lightnin' Hopkins, Muddy Waters and John Lee Hooker were some of my favorites. And I never learned how to play the piano. I'm sorry, Mommy, that we couldn't agree on my music instrument.

More importantly, I can most likely thank You, Lord, for steering my life away from the rock band epidemic that blossomed during the years that my guitar playing would have seriously begun—the 1950s and 1960s.

After a while, the situation changed. It was 1958. I was sixteen years old, and all my money needs were taken care of at that time. I had a regular job, doing work that I enjoyed, lots of friendly people around. Every day was another gift from the Lord.

Then suddenly, one day, it happened. "Turn off the lights and lock the doors," my boss told me. It was 1960, F. W. Woolworth Company, Marshall, Texas, and the lunch counter sit-ins had begun.

Ugly expressions, "getting back at you," mean, vengeful looks, some people from out of town all dressed up in their Sunday clothes, taking up as many seats as possible at the lunch counter.

The waitress was terrified, as were many of the customers. And thankfully, a riot did not happen, although a very angry group of white men soon arrived.

And what was accomplished on that day? Friendships were prevented or destroyed, lifelong enemies were created. Disgusting, frightful impressions were made. Suspicious behavior. What will happen next? Did someone have a dream? Was this the dream?

Martin Luther King day is a yearly celebration. Does anyone honor his work as a Baptist minister? Does teaching people about Jesus Christ and "loving your neighbor as much as yourself" have anything to do with a rude, gang-style takeover of someone's dinner table?

And is close seating among strangers proven to be a successful means of transmitting infectious disease? Is eating a lot of fast food good your health? Was this event a valuable prize that was won? There are a lot of serious questions to think about here.

"But he can't play football. His family doesn't have much money, and he's not all cute and talkative and popular. What a worthless boy he is. Let's bully him and embarrass him. Won't that be fun?"

Where did these common values and ideas come from over the years? How often were they practiced and exhibited in public schools?

One of my best friends was denied a college education. He confided with me at a later time that he had failed the entrance test that was required by the school for him to be admitted.

How sad. Then before long, another well-known acquaintance had a very similar experience. Now what was the matter here? It was hard to understand how neither of these two boys could get into college. Both of them appeared to be intelligent, healthy, and having a very positive hope to move ahead in life. And they had one special thing in common: they were star players on our high school football team.

If you didn't do your homework and couldn't pass your tests, don't worry. You can still move on to the next grade level and get a diploma from the high school, because you looked so good and did so many wonderful things on that football field. This rumor was often heard.

My opportunity was unique and another gift from God in my life. I was in a position to bestow on the governor of Texas, Mark White, one of the highest honors in freemasonry, the Lamar Medal, for his "no pass, no play" law that he pushed through the legislature. The football families of Texas would hate him for that, but it was a very wise and farsighted effort by him.

When I introduced the governor at that special event, I compared him to another hero of mine, Governor Sam Houston, who was hated and removed from office for his personal extra efforts, traveling around Texas, begging the public and local leaders not to get involved with the Southern Confederacy in the Civil War.

"Do the day's work"—that was the theme of Sir William Osler's speech to the graduating class at Yale University in 1913.

How many times have I thanked the Lord for the day that I accidentally picked up Dr. Osler's wise advice to those students.

From his own life experience, he had learned how easy it is for young students to become distracted by numerous powerful attractions while they are trying to complete their basic studies for a degree.

His study recommendations and his great faith in God became a very important guide throughout my college years, my career, and the rest of my life. Once again, I thank You, Lord.

Mama paid the owner fifty dollars, and I drove away in my own personal car. It was a very tired 1940 Ford coupe, but I was thrilled to get it. The year of this purchase was about 1958.

Author during high school years, 1958-60 (hotrod
cars, and rock stars and styles, etc)

"Forty Fords" had earned a reputation over the years for speed, styling, and cheap, dependable transportation. But the original engine was very much in need of repair or replacement.

As a fan of old car restoration and modifications, I ordered the necessary adapter parts and upgraded the engine to a 1954 Oldsmobile V-8 out of a wrecked car. (Many thanks to the Lord, and also a big thank-you to another friend, Henry, who provided much-needed help with this project.)

What fun, what power, and what dependable performance. It was a very special vehicle for me to drive from my home in Marshall, Texas, to mechanics school in St Louis, Missouri, in 1965.

Auto mechanics would eventually become one of the foundations of my lifework, which generally involved some kind of troubleshooting, problem solving, and customer service.

And where did I get the work ethic? Romantic movie stars from the 1940s and later had a big influence on me. But I had basic "farmboy" knowledge too. And I knew that once all that romantic action started, babies could soon arrive, and some good paychecks had better start arriving too.

Our Father…deliver us from evil. (Matthew 6:13)

As a young boy, listening to Mammaw, I could not forget how young men were called to serve in war times, or drafted, and had no say in what or where or how they would serve.

So on July 3, 1962, I joined the army. The result was that the Lord rescued me from a terrible fate in Vietnam and a boring, miserable life being married to the wrong person and/or working at a job that I hated so I could be exempt from military service.

Outstanding Soldier Award, the Good Conduct Medal, and an honorable discharge after three years as a radar operator on a Nike missile base in the New York Air Defense Command during the Cuban Missile Crisis. And education benefits (money for college) from the Veterans Administration after my three years of service were completed.

(Sp4 Jackson, 1965)

Thank You, Lord, and thank you, Mammaw, for the encouragement to go ahead and enlist in the army.

But now what? What would my future be? For a long time I had been interested in mechanics.

Bailey Technical School in St. Louis, Missouri, was my next stop.

But my education was not complete. The mechanics school was great, but I was hungry for more. How about some liberal arts courses at the university?

But first I needed to get back to Panola Junior College in Carthage, Texas, where I had made poor grades and took some more courses, made some good grades so I could transfer to the University of Texas.

It worked, English, Spanish, Ancient Greek, art history, Shakespeare, biology, philosophy, world history, government, speech, etc. and finishing with a business degree, BBA, with a major in management. It was an adventure that I will never forget and a blessing that I will always give thanks for.

Graduation from UT, 1974

Remembering that going for a good education is important, how Moses was educated by the Pharaoh's daughter in Egypt, and how the apostle Paul studied there too. The blessings of a good education for both of these men is very evident in their words to everyone from the Bible.

This suggests another question: where should a good education begin? Without a doubt, a good education should, of course, start with learning how to read and write and use a dictionary.

Then as one becomes proficient at this, to carefully read through the King James Bible from beginning to end, thinking about what it says and taking notes and remembering the main points that are important.

A proper Sunday school experience can help this process get started while we are still children. And some good sermons as we mature can also inspire us to continue on this great pathway.

Then after this serious Bible study, we are prepared to move on to the other areas of advanced learning and topics of interest for liberal arts, science, mathematics, and other subjects.

As I worked my way through my career choices, it was 1968, and what should I study next? Do I prepare for an office job? Or should I try out my mechanic training? Why not go to Alaska? They probably need some mechanics there, and it would be a good place to get some experience.

Alaska was only the first step in a beautiful time of interesting work, amazing scenery, and fascinating people. Oil field mechanics in Alaska and later in Dubai, with stops in New Orleans, London, Beirut, Ankara, and Iran. I was a tourist with a toolbox. Isn't God's world amazing and beautiful? Yes, I can testify to that.

What can you do with a glacier? Are you able to use it for something? It's big, and it's right there in front of you, frozen and secured in its place until next spring, when "breakup" occurs, the temperature drops, and it floats away.

Growler is another name that is used by the local people for a small glacier because it makes a loud scraping or growling noise when it is rubbing against other glaciers.

Every year when the temperature warms up and the ocean is not frozen, the small glaciers come floating in toward Alaska from Greenland. Then when the temperature drops, the ocean freezes around them, and they become locked in place until the next breakup in the springtime.

But the University of Alaska devised a way to keep growlers from floating away. They started pumping seawater from below the layer of ice. They pumped it up on top of the glacier while it was frozen in place.

Layer after layer was pumped and frozen until the additional weight caused the glacier to sink down onto the ocean floor. Then it would not float away and could be used as a temporary platform for an oil drilling rig or other purposes.

Yes, I flew in a Bell Jet Ranger helicopter to the glacier and worked on the diesel-powered water pump that was lifting the water through nine feet of ice. My employer during those times was Craig-Taylor Equipment Company in Fairbanks, Alaska.

Heavy Equipment Mechanic, Jim, Alaska 1969

And how about a wife for me? There were several females along the way that might have been a good choice. But I didn't think that I was ready to settle down. And I hadn't yet learned to ask the Lord to help me find a mate.

> And the Lord God said, It is not good that the
> man should be alone. (Genesis 2:18)

And being a daddy had never been important to me. Then I met and married a woman who could not have a baby. And I was told that if I had my own child, they would have birth defects. Was I being protected from one of the most heartbreaking experiences that a person can have?

Missing my farming past, I decided to combine my mechanic training with farm equipment sales at a dealership. This brought lasting friendships with some hardworking, kindhearted people whom I'll never forget. Isn't friendship a great gift from above? There's no doubt in my mind that it is.

The crops were beautiful, and sunny, rainy days came like the Bible says. And I was in my place, waking early every day, going hard and serious. Harvest would be coming soon, repairs would be needed, the days would be long but rewarding, and sleep would be very much needed.

My early years were full of cowboy stories. I saw myself living my life on horseback. And my great-grandfather was active in the Masonic Lodge. So being president of the Mustang Owners Club of Austin in 1983 and Worshipful Master of University Lodge in 1992 seemed to be tailor-made for me. Both were gifts from God during the years when my machinery career was coming to a sad end. They were some of those very special gifts:

> Above all that we can ask or think. (Ephesians 3:20)

Many people can send huge thank-you notes to the Lord for helping them during trials and hard times. I am one of those people.

Teddy was the name of our family mule. He had started standing up all the time, even when he was sleeping. It was a trait that horse and mule owners had learned about. When these animals began to have difficulty getting up from sleep, usually because of advanced age, they start sleeping while they are standing up.

Then one day, it happened. Teddy had an apparent heart attack, gave out one last loud bray, fell over, and died. He had been a wonderful family member, whether pulling the plow or the wagon with a load of people and their belongings. What a sad day it was.

Very close relationships with mules, horses, and other animals were a tradition and a blessing of the times of my ancestors who lived on the farm. Your animals knew what your schedule was and behaved accordingly.

If grandpa was walking too slowly when taking Teddy to the barn for his lunch, Teddy would start nudging grandpa's back to make him walk faster.

My own personal attraction to horses was greatly enhanced by my ownership of a sporty vehicle that was named after a horse, and not just any horse but a wild one, a 1966 Ford Mustang.

This attraction was fueled even more by my membership in a car club and finally becoming president of the Mustang Owners Club of Austin. Did I get to meet Carrol Shelby? Yes. Did I have a lot of fun? Yes and yes again and again. Many, many thanks to You, Lord.

The author with his "pony" 1996

So what is Freemasonry all about, anyway?

The Masonic Lodge is a very old organization. For many centuries, it has focused on biblical teachings for those who are not able to read, study, and apply God's guidance in their lives.

These "students" are basically good folks, but for various reasons, they have a communication problem with the Bible. So the lodge requires them to memorize the basic concepts which the scriptures are based on and tests their proficiency in this before letting them advance through the Masonic degrees.

The author wearing Masonic apron, 1992

For me, personally, it inspired me to get serious about reading and studying the King James Bible. I will always give a big thank-you to the Lord for that special inspiration.

In 1995, my first wife, Barbara, was diagnosed with terminal cancer. We had been married for over twenty years. Her final days were rough; the pain was terrible. My job was to make her as comfortable as possible.

Author's first wife, Barbara Lou Pierpont Jackson, 1992

Helplessness, grief, and emotions of the worst kind all crowded into each day. Two weeks before she died, she called me into her room and had me witness her request to Jesus Christ to forgive all her sins and come into her life. It's one of the happiest memories that I have.

Grief can kill you. I thought for a while that my life was over. But I have always believed that life is precious. So I would ask Jesus to help me every time my grief was bad. Numerous times I did this, and each time after about thirty minutes, I would start to feel happy.

The Lord is there when we need Him. I am living proof of that.

Having difficulty with my career, agriculture going away from central Texas, dealerships closing, getting laid off, getting older, unable to run hard all day long, too young to retire. What to do next?

Jesus Christ recycled me. And I still can't believe it. I was hired by the older worker program from the Department of Labor. I got retrained in the computer field, went to work for Unisys Corp., joined Christian Single Adults, and met and married a single mom with two young daughters. Yes, I was recycled.

The author with Bessie, Debra and their mother, Sue, 1999

What is fun here in this world, anyway? How could suddenly driving two little girls to school every day be fun? But it was. And how could driving them and their mother to Sunday school and church every week be fun? But it was.

And how could cooking, grocery shopping, housework, daddy and husband activities plus a new career as a computer technician all suddenly be fun? But it very much was. Another big thank-you, Lord.

So what is going on now?

Another birthday passed by, and now I'm eighty-one-years old. Still a member of the Baptist Church, praying and reading the King James Bible every day. Been through it about four or five times, from cover to cover. Still doing some computer work.

Still enjoying my old car hobby. Still handing out my tract, "Go Out with Joy," still witnessing and sharing my testimony with others. I owe a great debt to our heavenly Father and our Lord and Savior, Jesus Christ.

1966 Ford, Country Sedan, 390c

Author in his 1966 Ford

Next Step: A Daily Prayer

Lord Jesus, please forgive all my sins. I forgive everyone who has hurt me and wronged me, and I forgive myself and please hear this prayer:

Our Father who art in heaven, hallowed be thy name, Thy kingdom come, Thy will be done on earth as it is in heaven. Give us this day our daily bread and forgive us our sins as we forgive those who trespass against us. Lead us not into temptation but deliver us from evil, for Thine is the kingdom and the power and the glory, forever and ever. Amen.

And please give our love and our thanks to God the Father for letting us come here for a while and be a part of and enjoy His marvelous works and for heaven and for sending You, Jesus. A big thank-you to You, Lord, for dying on the cross, for sending the Holy Spirit and the angels to help us while we are here, and for taking away our sins so we can go to heaven.

Please stay with us, Lord, and help us with our choices and let us have wisdom, knowledge, understanding, instruction, and correction.

Jesus, we love You. Thank You for the King James Bible and thank You for the special efforts that are made preparing our dreams, where You tell us what to do or not to do. Thank You so much for those.

Thank You for friendship, love, and affection and for all our blessings. Please let us walk with You. In Your name, we pray, amen.

—Jim Jackson

About the Author

Jim Jackson is a white native male Texan who generally has conservative views and believes that Jesus Christ is a much more personal savior than we realize and is seated next to our heavenly Father, who is doing what He has always done. His life has been greatly blessed, and he hopes to share what he has learned from experience and Bible study for eighty-one years.

9 7 9 8 8 9 1 1 2 5 1 6 2